EMMANUEL JOSEPH

The Abstract Market, Monetizing the Untapped Potential of Non-Monetary Economies

Copyright © 2025 by Emmanuel Joseph

All rights reserved. No part of this publication may be reproduced, stored or transmitted in any form or by any means, electronic, mechanical, photocopying, recording, scanning, or otherwise without written permission from the publisher. It is illegal to copy this book, post it to a website, or distribute it by any other means without permission.

First edition

This book was professionally typeset on Reedsy.
Find out more at reedsy.com

Contents

1. Chapter 1 — 1
2. Chapter 1: The Hidden Wealth of Non-Monetary Economies — 3
3. Chapter 2: The Psychology of Value Exchange — 5
4. Chapter 3: Case Studies of Non-Monetary Economies — 7
5. Chapter 4: The Role of Technology in Bridging Economies — 9
6. Chapter 5: The Ethics of Monetizing Non-Monetary Economies — 11
7. Chapter 6: Designing Hybrid Economic Models — 13
8. Chapter 7: The Social Impact of Monetizing Non-Monetary... — 14
9. Chapter 8: The Future of Work in a Hybrid Economy — 15
10. Chapter 9: The Role of Education in Shaping the Invisible... — 16
11. Chapter 10: The Global Implications of Monetizing... — 17
12. Chapter 11: Overcoming Barriers to Monetization — 18
13. Chapter 12: A Vision for the Future — 19

1

Chapter 1

Introduction

In a world where financial transactions dominate our daily lives, there exists a parallel economy that operates quietly, often unnoticed, yet holds immense potential. This is the invisible market—a vast network of exchanges that thrive on barter, time banks, skill-sharing, and community-based systems where money is not the primary medium of exchange. From rural villages to bustling urban neighborhoods, people have long relied on these non-monetary systems to meet their needs, build relationships, and sustain their communities. These economies are built on trust, reciprocity, and shared values, offering a glimpse into a different way of organizing human interaction and resource distribution.

The invisible market is not a new phenomenon. Throughout history, societies have engaged in non-monetary exchanges to survive and thrive. What is new, however, is the growing recognition of these systems as untapped reservoirs of economic value. In an era marked by financial instability, environmental challenges, and widening inequality, the invisible market offers a resilient and sustainable alternative. It challenges the conventional notion that value can only be measured in monetary terms, inviting us to rethink how we define wealth and prosperity.

This book, *The Invisible Market: Monetizing the Untapped Potential of Non-Monetary Economies*, seeks to explore the hidden potential of these systems and how they can be integrated into the global economy. It is not merely an academic exercise but a practical guide to understanding and harnessing the power of non-monetary exchanges. By examining real-world examples, psychological principles, and technological innovations, we aim to uncover strategies for monetizing these economies without compromising their core values.

However, the journey to monetize the invisible market is not without its challenges. It requires a delicate balance between preserving the social and cultural fabric that sustains these systems and introducing mechanisms that allow them to scale and thrive in a globalized world. Ethical considerations, technological limitations, and resistance to change are just some of the barriers that must be addressed. Yet, the rewards are immense: a more inclusive, equitable, and sustainable economy that benefits individuals, communities, and societies at large.

As we embark on this exploration, we invite you to open your mind to the possibilities that lie beyond traditional economic paradigms. The invisible market is not just an alternative system; it is a testament to human ingenuity and the power of collaboration. By understanding and embracing its potential, we can create a future where value is not confined to monetary transactions but is enriched by the diverse ways in which we connect, share, and support one another. This book is a call to action—a challenge to see the invisible, to recognize its worth, and to unlock its transformative power.

2

Chapter 1: The Hidden Wealth of Non-Monetary Economies

In a world driven by financial transactions, there exists an invisible market—a vast network of exchanges that operate outside the realm of money. These non-monetary economies thrive on barter, time banks, skill-sharing, and community-based systems where value is created and exchanged without the need for currency. From rural villages to urban neighborhoods, people have long relied on these systems to meet their needs, often without realizing their economic potential.

The invisible market is not a new concept. Historically, communities have traded goods, services, and labor to sustain themselves. What is new, however, is the growing recognition of these systems as untapped reservoirs of economic value. In an era where traditional markets are increasingly volatile, the invisible market offers a stable and resilient alternative.

Yet, the challenge lies in understanding how to monetize these systems without disrupting their intrinsic value. The invisible market is built on trust, reciprocity, and social bonds—elements that are difficult to quantify but essential to its functioning. To harness its potential, we must first appreciate its complexity and the cultural nuances that sustain it.

This chapter explores the foundational principles of non-monetary economies, highlighting their historical significance and contemporary relevance. It sets the stage for a deeper exploration of how these systems can be integrated into the global economy, creating new opportunities for growth and innovation.

The invisible market is not just an economic phenomenon; it is a testament to human ingenuity and adaptability. By understanding its dynamics, we can unlock a wealth of opportunities that have long been overlooked.

3

Chapter 2: The Psychology of Value Exchange

At the heart of the invisible market lies a fundamental question: What makes people value something enough to exchange it? Unlike monetary economies, where price serves as a universal measure of value, non-monetary systems rely on subjective perceptions of worth. A loaf of bread might be worth an hour of labor in one context, but in another, it could be valued for the emotional comfort it provides.

This chapter delves into the psychology of value exchange, examining how individuals and communities assign worth to goods and services. It explores the role of trust, reputation, and social capital in facilitating exchanges, as well as the emotional and cultural factors that influence decision-making.

One of the key insights is that value in non-monetary economies is often relational rather than transactional. People are more likely to engage in exchanges with those they know and trust, creating a network of interdependence that strengthens community bonds. This relational aspect is both a strength and a challenge when it comes to monetization.

The chapter also examines the concept of "invisible currencies," such as time, skills, and social influence, which play a crucial role in non-monetary economies. These currencies are fluid and context-dependent, making them difficult to standardize but rich with potential for innovation.

By understanding the psychology of value exchange, we can begin to design systems that bridge the gap between non-monetary and monetary economies, creating hybrid models that leverage the strengths of both.

4

Chapter 3: Case Studies of Non-Monetary Economies

From the time banks of Japan to the barter networks of rural India, non-monetary economies take many forms around the world. This chapter presents a series of case studies that illustrate the diversity and adaptability of these systems. Each example highlights the unique ways in which communities create and exchange value without relying on money.

One case study focuses on the "Fureai Kippu" system in Japan, where individuals earn credits by providing care to the elderly. These credits can be saved, traded, or transferred to family members in other regions, creating a decentralized network of care that complements the formal healthcare system.

Another example explores the "Jugaad" economy in India, where resourcefulness and ingenuity drive informal exchanges of goods and services. From repurposing discarded materials to sharing agricultural equipment, these practices demonstrate the resilience and creativity of non-monetary systems.

The chapter also examines digital platforms like TimeRepublik and Bunz, which facilitate skill-sharing and barter in urban settings. These platforms show how technology can amplify the reach and impact of non-monetary economies, making them accessible to a global audience.

Through these case studies, the chapter underscores the adaptability of non-monetary economies and their potential to address pressing social and economic challenges.

5

Chapter 4: The Role of Technology in Bridging Economies

Technology has the power to transform the invisible market, making it more visible and accessible to a wider audience. This chapter explores how digital platforms, blockchain, and artificial intelligence can be leveraged to monetize non-monetary economies while preserving their core values.

Digital platforms like Local Exchange Trading Systems (LETS) and time banks have already demonstrated the potential of technology to facilitate non-monetary exchanges. By creating transparent and efficient systems for tracking transactions, these platforms enhance trust and accountability.

Blockchain technology offers another promising avenue for monetization. By creating decentralized ledgers that record exchanges of value, blockchain can provide a secure and transparent framework for non-monetary economies. Smart contracts, for example, could automate exchanges based on predefined criteria, reducing the need for intermediaries.

Artificial intelligence can also play a role in analyzing patterns of exchange and identifying opportunities for monetization. By understanding how value flows through non-monetary systems, AI can help design hybrid models that integrate monetary and non-monetary elements.

However, the chapter also cautions against over-reliance on technology, emphasizing the importance of preserving the human connections that underpin non-monetary economies. Technology should serve as a tool, not a replacement, for the social bonds that make these systems thrive.

6

Chapter 5: The Ethics of Monetizing Non-Monetary Economies

Monetizing the invisible market raises important ethical questions. How do we ensure that the process of monetization does not erode the social and cultural values that sustain non-monetary economies? This chapter explores the ethical considerations involved in integrating these systems into the global economy.

One concern is the risk of commodifying relationships that are based on trust and reciprocity. When exchanges are assigned a monetary value, there is a danger that they will become transactional rather than relational, undermining the very essence of non-monetary economies.

Another issue is the potential for exploitation. Without proper safeguards, monetization could lead to the extraction of value from vulnerable communities, exacerbating inequalities rather than addressing them.

The chapter also examines the role of governance in ensuring that monetization is carried out ethically. This includes creating frameworks that protect the rights of participants, promote transparency, and ensure that benefits are distributed equitably.

Ultimately, the chapter argues that monetization must be approached with care and respect for the cultural and social contexts in which non-monetary economies operate. By prioritizing ethical considerations, we can create models that enhance rather than diminish the value of these systems.

7

Chapter 6: Designing Hybrid Economic Models

The future of the invisible market lies in hybrid economic models that combine the strengths of monetary and non-monetary systems. This chapter explores how such models can be designed to create sustainable and inclusive economies.

One approach is to create dual-currency systems, where traditional money coexists with alternative currencies like time credits or skill tokens. These systems allow individuals to participate in both monetary and non-monetary exchanges, providing greater flexibility and resilience.

Another strategy is to integrate non-monetary economies into existing markets. For example, businesses could accept time credits as payment for goods and services, creating new revenue streams while supporting community-based exchanges.

The chapter also discusses the role of policy in enabling hybrid models. Governments can play a key role by recognizing and regulating alternative currencies, providing incentives for businesses to participate, and investing in infrastructure that supports non-monetary exchanges.

By designing hybrid models that leverage the best of both worlds, we can create economies that are more equitable, sustainable, and adaptable to the challenges of the 21st century.

8

Chapter 7: The Social Impact of Monetizing Non-Monetary Economies

Monetizing the invisible market has the potential to create significant social impact, from reducing poverty to strengthening community bonds. This chapter examines the ways in which monetization can address pressing social challenges.

One of the most promising aspects of monetization is its ability to create new opportunities for marginalized communities. By formalizing non-monetary exchanges, individuals who are excluded from traditional markets can gain access to resources and income.

Monetization can also strengthen social cohesion by providing a framework for recognizing and rewarding contributions that are often overlooked. For example, caregiving and volunteer work could be compensated through alternative currencies, acknowledging their value to society.

However, the chapter also highlights the risks of unintended consequences, such as the potential for monetization to create new forms of inequality or disrupt existing social structures.

By carefully considering the social impact of monetization, we can design systems that enhance well-being and promote inclusive growth.

9

Chapter 8: The Future of Work in a Hybrid Economy

As hybrid economic models gain traction, the nature of work is likely to undergo significant changes. This chapter explores how monetizing non-monetary economies could reshape the labor market and create new opportunities for workers.

One possibility is the rise of "micro-entrepreneurship," where individuals monetize their skills and assets through non-monetary exchanges. For example, someone with a spare room could earn time credits by hosting travelers, creating a new source of income.

Another trend is the growing importance of soft skills like empathy, collaboration, and creativity, which are highly valued in non-monetary economies. As these skills become more recognized, they could play a central role in the future of work.

The chapter also examines the potential for hybrid models to address issues like job insecurity and income inequality. By providing multiple pathways for earning and exchanging value, these systems could create a more resilient and inclusive labor market.

Ultimately, the future of work in a hybrid economy will require a shift in mindset, as individuals and organizations learn to navigate the complexities of both monetary and non-monetary systems.

10

Chapter 9: The Role of Education in Shaping the Invisible Market

Education plays a crucial role in unlocking the potential of the invisible market. This chapter explores how educational initiatives can empower individuals and communities to participate in and benefit from non-monetary economies.

One key area is financial literacy, which can help people understand the value of alternative currencies and how to use them effectively. By teaching individuals how to navigate hybrid economic models, education can bridge the gap between monetary and non-monetary systems.

Another focus is on fostering skills that are essential for non-monetary exchanges, such as communication, negotiation, and problem-solving. These skills not only enhance participation in the invisible market but also have broader applications in life and work.

The chapter also highlights the importance of community-based education, where knowledge is shared through informal networks and peer-to-peer learning. This approach aligns with the principles of non-monetary economies, emphasizing collaboration and mutual support.

By investing in education, we can create a more inclusive and equitable invisible market, where everyone has the opportunity to contribute and benefit.

11

Chapter 10: The Global Implications of Monetizing Non-Monetary Economies

The invisible market is not confined to local communities; it has global implications that extend far beyond individual exchanges. This chapter explores how monetizing non-monetary economies could reshape the global economy and address pressing global challenges.

One potential impact is the reduction of economic inequality. By creating new pathways for earning and exchanging value, monetization could empower marginalized communities and reduce disparities between rich and poor.

Another implication is the potential for non-monetary economies to contribute to environmental sustainability. Many non-monetary systems are inherently resource-efficient, relying on sharing, recycling, and repurposing rather than consumption.

The chapter also examines the role of international cooperation in supporting the growth of the invisible market. By sharing knowledge and best practices, countries can learn from each other and create a more interconnected and resilient global economy.

Ultimately, the global implications of monetizing non-monetary economies are vast and far-reaching, offering new possibilities for addressing some of the world's most pressing challenges.

12

Chapter 11: Overcoming Barriers to Monetization

While the potential of the invisible market is immense, there are significant barriers to monetization that must be addressed. This chapter explores the challenges and opportunities involved in overcoming these barriers.

One major challenge is the lack of infrastructure to support non-monetary exchanges. Without systems for tracking and valuing exchanges, it can be difficult to scale these economies and integrate them into the global market.

Another barrier is resistance to change, particularly from those who benefit from the status quo. Monetizing non-monetary economies requires a shift in mindset and a willingness to embrace new ways of thinking about value and exchange.

The chapter also examines the role of policy and regulation in overcoming barriers. Governments can play a key role by creating frameworks that support non-monetary economies, from recognizing alternative currencies to providing funding for innovation.

By addressing these barriers, we can unlock the full potential of the invisible market and create a more inclusive and sustainable global economy.

13

Chapter 12: A Vision for the Future

The invisible market represents a new frontier in economic innovation, offering untapped potential for growth, resilience, and social impact. This final chapter paints a vision for the future, where monetary and non-monetary economies coexist and complement each other.

In this future, individuals and communities have multiple pathways for creating and exchanging value, from traditional jobs to time banks and skill-sharing platforms. The boundaries between monetary and non-monetary systems blur, creating a more fluid and adaptable economy.

This vision is not without its challenges, but it is one that holds immense promise. By embracing the principles of trust, reciprocity, and collaboration that underpin non-monetary economies, we can create a world where everyone has the opportunity to thrive.

The invisible market is no longer invisible; it is a vital part of our economic landscape, offering new possibilities for innovation and growth. The journey to monetize this market is just beginning, and the opportunities are limitless.

Book Description

The Invisible Market: Monetizing the Untapped Potential of Non-Monetary Economies is a groundbreaking exploration of the hidden networks of exchange that operate outside the traditional financial system. This book delves into the world of barter, time banks, skill-sharing, and community-based economies, revealing how these systems create value without the need for money. From rural villages to urban neighborhoods, non-monetary economies have long been a cornerstone of human interaction, fostering trust, reciprocity, and resilience. Yet, their potential to transform the global economy has remained largely untapped—until now.

Through a blend of real-world case studies, psychological insights, and innovative strategies, this book uncovers the immense economic and social value of non-monetary systems. It examines how these economies function, the principles that sustain them, and the challenges of integrating them into a world dominated by monetary transactions. From the time banks of Japan to the barter networks of rural India, the book showcases diverse examples of non-monetary exchanges, highlighting their adaptability and relevance in addressing modern challenges such as inequality, environmental sustainability, and economic instability.

At its core, *The Invisible Market* is a call to rethink how we define value and wealth. It challenges the assumption that money is the only measure of economic success, offering instead a vision of a hybrid economy where monetary and non-monetary systems coexist and complement each other. The book explores how technology, policy, and education can bridge the gap between these systems, creating opportunities for innovation and growth while preserving the social bonds that make non-monetary economies so powerful.

However, the journey to monetize the invisible market is not without its complexities. The book addresses the ethical dilemmas, cultural sensitivities, and practical barriers that must be navigated to ensure that monetization enhances rather than undermines these systems. It emphasizes the importance of designing hybrid models that are inclusive, equitable, and sustainable, offering a roadmap for individuals, businesses, and policymakers to harness the potential of non-monetary economies.

The Invisible Market is more than just a book—it is a manifesto for a new economic paradigm. It invites readers to see beyond the limitations of traditional markets and to imagine a future where value is created and exchanged in ways that enrich our lives, strengthen our communities, and build a more resilient world. Whether you are an entrepreneur, a policymaker,

CHAPTER 12: A VISION FOR THE FUTURE

or simply someone curious about alternative economic systems, this book offers a fresh perspective and practical tools to unlock the untapped potential of the invisible market.

www.ingramcontent.com/pod-product-compliance
Lightning Source LLC
LaVergne TN
LVHW020508080526
838202LV00057B/6249